THE MAN IN THE BROWN SUIT

Copyright © 2018 John Kolchak
All rights reserved

Published by Ward Six Press
Los Angeles, CA USA
Design by Geraldine Baum

The Man in the Brown Suit
First printing, 2013
ISBN: 978-0984013029

wardsixpress.com

THE MAN IN THE BROWN SUIT

CONVERSATIONS WITH THE DEVIL ABOUT THE NEW WORLD

JOHN KOLCHAK

This book is dedicated to the Pan-Am building, which stood for many years as an icon of flight and an emblem of endless possibility...
until it was replaced by an insurance company.

PEEK- a -boo!

Scared you?

SUCKER!!!

You've been washing my ass in the bath-house your entire life!

Now I'm clean.

And you're old.

Now I get to keep the money

AND the bag!

So said the Devil.

I told him to shut his face.

The HELL you did!

Andrei comes up to me outside
the record store speaking in broken Russian
vulgarisms, like a Vulgar Boatman.

Fuck man, my bitch is pregnant...

So, what are you gonna do?

The fuck you think?
With the amount of dope I got in my system,
the thing's gonna come out
all deformed and shit.

I run into Andrei twenty
years later, the years didn't make
his Ukrainian Jewish nose any smaller.

We used to call him "Nose" in High School.

He tells me he's a gigolo now
and makes a lot of money servicing older ladies.

He's lying.

He's not even a Joe Buck.

A few years later I see him on the street,
"I just got out of prison" he says and
calls me the next day, and asks if he
could swing by. He arrives, pours a coffee mug
of my emergency cheap brandy, brags:

"Niggers never fucked me when I was in the can"
pours the rest of my booze into a McDonalds
styrofoam cup and gets on the N line.

His son died, my mother screamed, his only son,
he died!

I didn't know the son or the father.

Not Andrei, just some other unfortunate.

And that other guy, he was standing on
the platform in Times Square, waiting for
the train...

"Gimme a qwatah" So Vlad or Serge or Ivan
gives a quarter, the guy asks for more, and
when Vlad says that's all I've got, he's pushed
under the train.

A few years later, my mother sees him,
in a wheelchair with legs cut off, amputated,
drinking vodka from a milk carton, delirious.

We used to make Russian Salad for
the Russian Club.

Potatoes, pickles, mayonnaise…

We'd bring over food, and I would see
adults discussing things.
They were too busy fighting for human rights
or something like that…

Yea, by the waters of Manhattan was
where we sat down.
And there we wept when we
remembered Europe.

Out of captivity, we looked at
the Palisades Parkway,
chewing on big rotten fruit,
spitting out worms,
tongues cleaving our mouths.

Boo!

Oh all right, talk your bollocks...

THE MAN IN THE BROWN SUIT

New York would always leave me
broken hearted, and even though I've since
abandoned it for smoggier and greener
pastures, I must admit its soft brown light
has not departed, although
the Man in the Brown Suit appears in
dreams from time to time,
and came to me today.

It takes a while to notice that he's
cloven-hoofed and just when you have
thought you'd seen a tail, he quickly
switches his position on the chair,
turns on his charm and puts on airs,
and when you leave with this
old Mister Goodbar then know:
you're tempting fate. God save you if
you're strong enough to dodge
the outcome of so many,
for whom realization came too late.

I've beat him only slightly, and
the tables haven't turned, and I was
wretched and naïve with body cavities deformed,
and much like poor Ms Short who disappeared
into the Biltmore, I too can still be
found eviscerated by a familiar stranger:
The Man in the Brown Suit,
when memories are excavated.

Arriving in New York from
sun drenched Rome, where
there's another odd demon or angel
or some other thing unknown that
casts a special glow, provides a stunning light,
I wept in fear of buildings tall and frightening
and people small as ants
who scurried to and fro -
Dystopia before I knew that word, and
world was lit by lightning.

I cried each time that I went back,
forced to return to city full of fear and horror,
with all the horror stories that I'd heard
of ant people crushed under the tremendous
weight of their own hill.

The Man in the Brown Suit is quite a charmer.
In time I saw the tail and fearlessly
I'd try to wriggle myself out of his attempts
at molestation and yet this was my home,
the anthill my new nation,

And so I'd bend to him.

In time, though, his advances turned
more sinister and now with me
no longer meek, he'd try some new techniques
and prey upon the weak for me to see and
meanwhile whisper in my ear most
tempting and most filthy thoughts.

I tried to fight and not to fear and I sent flying
poet's walking stick into Old Filthy's face
which naturally went
right in the mirror.

I was lucky.

The Man in the Brown Suit sits
atop the Chrysler Building's spire
and with a power both demonic and divine
picks out his victims randomly and sees
which targets he shall pick.
The man can reap for miles.
They're there for him in spades, and
Old Nick never tires.

How soft and yellow light falls unto
Central Park or on the avenues
when day turns into night. That is when
well worn and deceitful wings that sprout
from his Brown Suit envelop you and
try to soothe your heartache
"It is home, after all…"

For me, no more!

I hope I've left for good, I pray
feet gripping mud and staying steadfast in LA.
The streets and avenues of brown New York
have taken on a different look

or so I've read or heard,
but I think cloven hoofed
Emperor of Atlantis had
just changed into another chocolate
suit and donned another shoe.

Memories change, some stay, some
fade but even those of us who
suffered from a childhood trauma
find in some recollections of the past
some joy or God knows what.
For me, I try to turn, look back without
turning to salt, and say the things that
matter are the ones that last.

What does it mean? A hollow dream.

The city's now transformed although its
light remains eternal and the same.
It brings you Christmas presents
of both joy and pain with a fake yule log
on the telly when in fact, you're freezing cold.
It is in vain to seek some comfort in the old
brown overcoat or in the ragged canopy of
New York sky or the
umbrella symphony on sidewalks.

How tempting is the light, supposed joy,
the noise, and nuzzled deep in its brown heart
how quickly one forgets how many
it destroys.

There are no angels on the balcony, the
trumpets are the sounds of taxicabs below.
They're stuck in snow, it's cold outside
and though you clutch each other, whisper
"It's just you and me",
the Man in the Brown Suit laughs
looking at you from the top of
World Trade Center, and grinning
teeth as yellow as the New York twilight,
lays naught to thoughts and plans
accordingly.

I'd like to see that man exposed
for once! To see the old brown suit now
hanging from a hanger, and yell out:
that old garment's just the
Emperor's new clothes!

But loyal subjects and a drove of such naïve
newcomers, don't wish to see the Old Man's
wrinkly skin so nakedly disclosed.
And some will win but tell me then,
how many more will dangle?

I've won for now, Old Satan.
So tempting with a big old apple.
I'm grateful for the fruit and all,
but not for the damnation
and the fall.

And when I visit you and pass by
my old playground, I feel a terrible,
lonely relief that now my only link to you is
twenty miles away and in a graveyard
where my mother rests and lays
and where I come to visit
and to weep.

I'll take that lonely place of crosses,
dew and sorrow so much more
gratefully than any of the Trojan
gifts from you. In fact, to boot,
I'll pray for anyone who chooses to accept
an invitation from an old false friend
who's cloaking all the horrors that one
can imagine:
the ones he's stored in
lint and memory filled pockets
of his old brown suit.

Then we adjusted blinds and blinders,

when feedbags were adjusted.

THE FINISH RACE

Some get a head start way before the whistle
or the starter gun, those are the ones
who'll have more fun, although
the finish line's what counts.
But finish is the same for all
when it is done.
We trot or rush
or gallop, wearing blinders.
Reverting back to carbon's the reward, there is
no medal, we all go back to universal stable.

Equine, ovine or bovine, some of us
start out with handicap,
holes in the heart are drilled by God:
a Picador up in the sky that lets out blood just
to enrage us further, and so the thinking's
always been – it's better him than I, and
matadors are always at advantage, while
blind with rage, the bull will charge at anything
that comes his way, horse, man, any one thing,
oh, any target. "Why was I born if it was just to
die?"

And now about the other horses without jobs,
the ones who do not help to kill, nor able bodied
for the race, or to do much at all,
well, those are us!

The ones who cannot handle the dressage
or laps we can't complete as
teeth grow long, the feet get weary and the
sack of oats becomes much harder to
digest or even chew.

So cheers, champagne, to lucky few!
A wave from box seats, extra feed bag double
stuffed, it helps forget that we will
all be snuffed and back to molecules.

For those of us who live outside the racetrack,
without the food and pampering and grooming
that it holds, we drag old carriages, drive hearses,
we work and trod and stand in wait, just
to be boiled down into soap
when we are no longer of use.

What to do then, what to say?
To weep and whinny, or shall we
pray and neigh?
You've all had head starts, bangtail,
trotter, mudder.
Years pass as fast as laps,
we know we can't catch up.

The Derby cup is nice to own while you're
around on earth. For those of us
in common stables, we've got a
different approach.

We not-so thoroughbreds sometimes
still try to buck when we are saddled,
but mostly we're too tired to do much
and you are far ahead.

Whipped to submission and exhausted,
defeated thanks to your head start,
we stick our noses in the feedbag.
We eat your oats while gagging from disgust.
We transport coffins, chew on indignation.
And each time opportunity does knock,
we try to kick the coachman in his legs.

And in his heart.

But we had fun in both mid-aged
and childhood revelry.

A Harlem of the mind!

ALEXANDER THE GRAPE

That was the silly name of the bodega from
which I would buy fruit flavoured ices.

Like a more famous European Son now quite
forgotten and dead be it in university or
fleabag, rotting, (rot is rot, who cares), the one
who scalded by the baked potato thought of new
devices: how to maintain both booze and
teaching others, how to write or so to speak, and
talked about Czar Nick, and helped soft
undergrowth to blossom, he had his baked
potato and I had my ices.

And like a European Son in my own right, in my
own turn, I'd run down to the shop for my own
treat, without icing, and make sure to be home
for dinner, and plus, we'd never bake potatoes.
That's not Russian. Spurious tales or
trying to assimilate? Not my concern.
Back to me, me, me:

So I would run between cars and buses,
with limited amount of time and run
back to the palace.
In fact that's what the building's name, etched on
the entrance was: "Palace".

A simple truce between King Alexander and our
atrocious abode.
He hands me treats and I retreat.

Pyrrhic victory at times,
when I'd be late for dinner.
Victory nonetheless, with grape popsicle in hand
and parents screaming.

Alexander the Grape! Running back past
the marquee for a movie set replaying Europe,
gunshots outside and islanders but don't
fret now, for here you're safe, and plus,
so many books, and you can look outside.
So I would play.

And Haven Avenue looked just like the
Palace Embankment, with Winter Palace
by Fort Lee somewhere just right across the
Hudson.

And Harlem looked just like
St Petersburg to me.

And piss stained streets and
shit stained sidewalks were ruins
of old former glory
which I had never seen but that's
how I would see them through my fantasy.
And yet they would not set me free, by far, for
unlike Mr Schwartz I would pick up

my boiled or fried potato, even if

it fell in dirt or if

the Czar's children would still
play with their balloons.

Who cares about them?

They'll be shot soon!

For in my mind, the rosy sunsets on the Hudson
still retain a rosy picture, and dreams still
play the sweetest tunes.

And when it's winter, instead of Hitler,
it will be February
who'll murder all the Junes.

Here we are, here are,
again in exile, this time in the sun.

Could be worse...

Could always be worse...

Where will I go?

Where can I go?

Bridge, bridge...

And I too dreamt of my Russian summers...

Summers in Moscow are quite brilliant.
The Yanks think we're Eskimos and wear
bear skins throughout the year. Sorry to
disappoint, it's actually quite hot and smoggy
in the summer, but I digress...

The way I dreamt was how I now dream
of New York, both in the past now.

But in the 110 film of the mind, even New Lands,
New Earths looked warmer
and more promising.

Just like from that pissoir of
Coney Island boardwalk, when
the ocean looked inviting and we
thought we could do anything!
Gallantly sidewalking, a book of poetry in the
front flap of the jacket,
a pint of whiskey in the ass pocket,
or poetry in mind.
Head in the trousers.
Cock in the clouds.
Blood in the panties.

We beat minds like percussion instruments.
We could not play the piano.

THE GREEN CUP IN LISTOPAD

Memories come and go. Some stick while
others at least pinprick next to those
that stab like sharpened butter knife.
The blade gets dull with time and there is effort
needed to dig into flesh that's not yet fully
sagged.

Sometimes the knives
and the remembrances give up.
One holds me still, and so I'll save 'til grave
the memory of a green cocoa cup in Listopad.

The word means literally 'falling leaves'.
For Czechs, November is the month,
for Croats it's October.
For Russians, it's all gloom, impending doom:
it's Listopad year round.
The leaves are always falling, we think
it's over when it starts.

My memories of Russia are so poor
that I'm amazed I can remember
that fall day. How red and yellow leaves
swirled right above our heads in frenzy,
my mother held my hand and said:
"It's Listopad!" and then we ran across
the square to catch a trolley bus.

We went to see a relative whose
name I can't remember, but I remember
the green cups.

It wasn't Uncle Peter, the one who stole a piano
from the Austrians when rolling with
Red Army into Linz and dragged it
back a thousand miles east.

Not Uncle Tikhon, the electrician who spent
ten years in gulags for coming late to work,
when country was the fiefdom of a beast.

Not Aunt Maria, she drank herself to death.

Not Aunts Fatiha, Fatima or
Fatma, my dad's three sisters, none of them,
just like in the play, managed to make it
to Moskva. Instead they disappeared
somewhere in Central Asia.

I don't know who we went
to visit that fall day, and with my
mother dead, now I will never know.
What's left in mind is Listopad, how
leaves flurried like snowflakes, and
carousel of colours whipped up by the
wind, as if God chose to throw
some fancy by our side before the dark
set in, to lighten up the sterile city.

The colours smashed into our
faces and much in Russian style they
laughed and wept, as if they said
"I know I'm dying but don't you see
how beautiful I look?
From useless green, I turn orange and red!
Winter's ahead but now let's fiddle like the
grasshopper - while we still can!"

My mother laughed and hand in hand we
ran through the park path and caught
the trolley bus in time. I don't remember
who we went to see.

We drank hot cocoa
out of green porcelain cups.

In between thinking of Hands Across America,
or the biennial
or losing virginity in Brooklyn
or wandering along the waters,
seeing tall ships coming in behind
that reminder that, us maniacs,
we finally did it.

I recall the hit man named
the Polack, the Ice Man.

So easily returning to suburban home
after disemembering and butchering
and playing god.
Returning to his
New Jersey and
washing off blood.

Note:
he lived in Jersey,
not New York.

But there's delicious pizza
down the block from the
Gemini Lounge.

You provide the love,
I'll provide the suffering.

You provide the bread,
I'll provide the longing.

THE WARREN

We're thrust into the world as blind as rabbits,
as meek and tiny creatures struggling to see.
Not leverets who pop out of the womb with
open eyes but pink and squirming, screaming
"What the shit?!"
Hell, even Hitler suckled on his mommy's tit,
or so I'd like to think.
I'll give him benefit of doubt.

Most any parent, even monsters actually,
will try to build a home, however feeble
it may be. A nest that comforts
tiny offspring with the warmth of
straw or hay or fur. What happens to
the nest in time when parents die?
Was all the comfort just a lie?

Do frail and gentle creatures always hunted
dream of a return? Tall, tough and stupid humans
like myself certainly do, in times of pain, yearn to
come back to nest, or even womb, at least for a
look-see, but what is it we seek?
To know what's happened to the warren?
It overgrew with moss because security was
trumped by instinct to be free.

God blessed and cursed us with
the melancholy of reflection.

Memories blaze with whispers
of eternity and stasis.

They also leave us shivering outside
a burrow that's been overgrown with weeds.

The entrance to the hole's closed up with dirt
and deep inside, a family of rats is busy chewing
the foundation which the rabbits built, laying
down nests in place for their own filthy young
which multiply in spades and give
fuckall about your house or your remains.

In vain we sit outside the tunnel to the warren
of our minds and only wish that we could enter
once again and hide inside a quilt.
But what's inside?

As I just said, if warren hasn't yet collapsed,
nothing but rats. And on our end, nothing
but yearning for the comfort of the past.

Here we have fruit flies.
In New York we had rats.

Here we have drive-bys.
In New York the methods used
were old school: baseball bats.

East coast was six hours from
Europe, here it's ten.
It makes us feel we're closer
to Japan than old brown London.

And yet still in the night,
despite the "benefits",
a little mite, a little midge
finds it's way in our ears and
whispers gently while gnawing
through and through inside
and asks, while chewing
"Don't you miss me and my rot?
I know you do!"

"There's a yearning in nature today" you said
to me on the Fifth Avenue bus as I stared out
and imagined castles.

Little did I imagine then that nature,
in order to continue, only
yearns for the season of rain and death.

And this was in spring, to boot, perhaps
in cruelest month, and I went on my way
to sprout and gone on to eat wormes and
swich wretchedness.

I learned by example from brids.

I saw it recently, even the rot is
gone. City planning has done
one hell of a job, spent oceanfulls
of lipstick on the pig that can't
fly straight and Rockaways just
rock away as if no one has noticed
the cardiectomy.

Where are we?

Where are we now, on the edge of the world?

And even Athens burns so we get
a tiny taste of exile.

But it has always been exile to me.

One continent on fire,
another drowned in mire.

And all of us stuck in nonsense.

ARABIAN NIGHTS

One thousand and one nights were in fact,
oh more or less, actually less and
if you do the math, Schecherezade
had just under three years to save her skin.
It was around three years from start to end with
you, but that was opposite:
race towards the end.

Hell-bent running toward the end.

I found a paperback in French up on the shelf,
the title: "Les mille et une nuits".
I never read the tales, the cover
scared me as a child.
Monstrous fish and monstrous folks and
something I had no desire to read or see.

I looked at the book's cover and I felt myself
submerged in water, unable to breathe.
And then, a strange thing happened as the image
on the front of the French paperback in memory
all of sudden gave me calm.

It brought me back into the warren where the
monsters were just fairy tales of Sinbad, and not
the monsters that move in with us as
time and age advances.

These grown up boys have got big balls, oh quite
a pair, and they've got talons that will stick!

They curl up by your neck
and whisper "I ain't going anywhere"
and frolick when you're sick and wait
for proper moment.

But when I, scared of Sinbad's creatures, ran
and jumped into your bed,
I knew that I'd be safe.
No more, not anymore, not now,
and not until I'm dust like you.

Exposed, exposed... Not to Arabian Sea,
Persian Gulf or Indian Ocean... but to
the elements of mind and time. I'm stripped,
in nakedness or fear.

Tossing away clichés, I did indeed, often choose
a book by the cover. And though they do much
often cover just another. Odd, how the cover of a
book can hold associations.
Another one still makes me weep,
a simple drawing on the cover of Max Gorky's
stories. the sordid lullaby of some poor slut
who tells him
"Fuck me" and then "If you want,
I'll put a bag over my head", one more
"exposure" and how well described.
The tears of our besotted Russian nation.

Murderous, rotten race, and yet so soaked in
kindness, sometimes a marzipan sweet,
nauseating maudlin treat, and yet quite often
a really true desire for salvation.

Now back to business:
all of us know, even
Schecherezade that
sooner much than later, the scimitar will fall.
For some too late for some too young.
How did she escape her fate?
I can't remember now.
No matter, will just continue
moving forth.

Arabian, or Russian nights
are really quite a bore.

For all she did was to prolong the end.

And we all do the same.

Such are the tales,
such is the nature of the game.

RUSSIAN BATH

Memories suffocate us, some
even physically, and when you throw
in moisture, I think of all the heat
in that apartment since
abandoned, wherein now vermin thrive.

The long hot baths in winter, also your
Hamam, and in the summer it was
much like a sauna in its turn.
The dead are clean, the filth so
very much alive.

The Finns say build the sauna first, they'd
have a field day in New York: bath house is
already there and hardy Nordic Nazis can just
swap a jump in a cold lake for
humid velvet blanket of the night.

Oh cut me slack, it's not about stereotypes,
though they ring true. We're talking now
about the zoo, my case in point, the fact is
rats like moisture, and that's why when they're
perched up on their Heights,
and poised to jump down for the kill,
they do it quick, and when they've eaten
they survive.

Norwegian rats can kill a cow, or so I've heard,
and not to mention the black death and plague,

but stolid Norway isn't my
concern, forget the references to the dour torpor
of Scandinavia, it is the vermin that's my subject
and my game.
I mean the rats that come from blue sea
islands, who swim from
misery to misery and who are all so
predisposed to bite, and bite again.

How in the summer we all sat so merrily and
cooked in our own juice!
Just like a sauna or a Russian bath,
with all the stench and all the soot!
Merengue drowning out our words
of gulags, Dostoyevsky (don't fret he's coming
up), and all the memories of life and art,
with all the horrors, natch, to boot.

Those steaming New York summer nights
filled with such talk of poetry and literature and
geopolitics are but a memory for when the sauna
is dismantled and Ratus Carribeanus moves in
it does not amount to much, we know this now,
but wait...

I had another thought to ponder and another
tale to tell...

Whose nightmare was it about a
bathhouse filled with roaches
as a dream of hell?

A character from Dostoyevsky,
someone from Crime and Punishment,
(the punishment's the part I have a problem
with).
Besotted couches, mirrors, and the drunk black
man.

A broken mirror, nightmare works of fiction,
and dreams of things just hinted at by prophets
who talked so well over quotidian pain.
I struggle to recall the name...

Now I remember, vaguely, it was he!
That fat guy, that fat, smug bastard
Svidrigailov, who held on for dear
life, the one who raped the Marmeladovs'
daughter, if he existed and could see his
nightmare come to life, in the north end of
Manhattan, I wonder what he'd say?
He'd probably scream, as when I wished to
scream when I saw rats instead of roaches
as curtain closed and bathhouse suddenly grew
wings, lifted itself out of the trash and
into light, with I.V. bags and empty brandy
bottles, rubbish scattered, and then
the next day we saw Jacob's Ladders.

But vermin are not frightened of man's
presence, much less shadows.

Foundation stands. Truly a brick shithouse invulnerable to the fall, the buildings built like these are those that last....

...but there's that pesky little problem with the rats.

THE SILENT ANGEL

I used to say back in the
New York days, and this was actually
twice true, that there's a bridge outside
my window but I've nowhere to
drive to.

And now there's no more bridge, and while
I've got my motor car there aren't so
many places left to go which aren't far, and
close ones bore me, while the lucky ol' sun just
goes its merry way and keeps on burning.

And when it's six pm or seven and all the
dishes rinsed and the telephone calls
completed, I feel I'm chomping at the bit -
for something else is needed.

The Slavs say that when we are silent, a quiet
Angel flew on by and passed us over.
Well now it's over and we're quiet but
the heartache hardly ceases.
The devil shares his time
with angels in the silence.
Meanwhile,
when you fly by,
is when I fall to pieces.

THE SADDEST GIRL IN THE WORLD

Hard to define time, everything seems
as if it was just yesterday and I can't remember
what I had for breakfast, though I remember
now when I was too afraid to eat a peach.

Another aspect to it all is that some
are born quite old, some born too young,
some born too soon, and some were born
in cemetery too.

The last one I don't know how true, sometimes
I too feel stillborn, but I do know I've done
more than a bit of squandering on tears
and nicotine and ethanol and it
continues yet.

But looking back I recall vivid as
the nightfall of the boozy haze of yesterday, a
snowstorm we were snowed in, looking at your
panties with a drop of blood, the way
you spoke just of regret. Too much to bear,
too much to hold, when one's in cemetery born.

You may have been the saddest girl I ever
met, and made me sadder still,
a dead-end start to life of sex and the romantic
thrill.

"And when my mother dies, I will plant
sunflowers on her grave, they
turn their heads towards the sun..."

The saddest flower, the saddest girl in all the
world offers her Mother, passing
one generation down to next.

"The only place outside New York that I had
been to was Quebec.
We took a boat across the St Lawrence river, and
bought wild strawberries".

I do not know if sadness still persists for you.
I have a feeling that it does. I see you now, when
you're returning back home to your flat
on crosstown bus,
(you looked like Betsy but inside pure Travis) and
looking out at the falling autumn
in New York, I wonder if you ever will recall
just how you fell or chose to fall, or how when
everything became so damned fucked up,
just when you struggled to stand up.

I ordered a slice of apple pie with a
piece of American cheese melted on top.

You could have had anything you wanted.

THIS SPORTING LIFE

Whee whee whee!
We'd spend our youth in glee!
The beast lurks in the jungle but we cannot see
when he will pounce and ounce for ounce
it's better not to know, right?

Wrong. I struggle how to guess which one is
easier but all in all,
it's not a theme park after dark.
Existence's worth it's salt and
therefore something that is much more stark.
Allow me to explain...

Lights do not dim then fade.
They turn from candy colours of the ferris wheel
into fluorescents with a dash of
phosphorescent green, hospital viridescent
or sometimes hospital yellow.

For some the world's a stage, for some
it's nothing but carnival lights.
Performers know how to put on a show
even in the shadow of a crematorium at Belsen.

My mother's mother does this now.
Reads palms and flirts,
she's unaware her daughter's dead
and she can hardly recognize me.
I don't know if she can see.

And so, with age, the interstellar space
becomes wide open and deranged.

What dark or dusky or maybe
even totally blind future dangles taunting
by our eyes whereas before...

In Buchenwald I danced.
In Belsen I had pranced.
I slept in Sobibor
because there were so more, so
many places yet to see...
The one place that's too close to me
are the cold Isles of Solovki.

I mean no disrespect and hate no
one to such extent, the
weirdness is the truth.

We dance, we prance, we beg
the dance floor not to close, not
to shut down...

It's Shiva's dance, it never ceases.
Kaleidoscope for when we're young,
and neon bulbs and green and blue
and rather childlike you have to wear diapers
while a fat Haitian cleans your ass.
Odd how so quickly that the days and years have
passed, ne c'est pas?

With the development of blindness
(my biggest fear) I'm told the loss of sight
is gradual (although quite real).
Much like a sunset.
That's what I read from Borges.

Sightless or not, the carousel will never
ever really break.
It's just we're taken
to the kiddie section while we wait as
others buy a fare and
we still wish to jump and
hold the plastic horse, but
we're no longer let to do that and
thus spend our toothless
end in yellow corridors
with our lives
painted on walls
in colours of despair.

A sporting life is what it is, and when
the technicolor canopy is dropped
the ones alive go home,
turn back and wonder
"Did we even see the show?'"
We'll have to wait to know.

STRANGE HOW THE INTERLUDE IS SHORT

I struggle for a word and try to guess,
it means: "where is it now"? And I confess
I have no word for it. If I was young
I would have made one up myself.

I feel a loss for words, a loss for loss
and loss for magic. The feeling leaves
a burning in the brain and mixed with pain, again
a hole comes back, a yearning for some
magic to return, for in the playground of the
mind, the sobering of time lays waste to wonder
in between flashing lights of God the Father.

Oh how we screamed and shit our pants, that too
but that's because when we were kids we
knew what's bollocks and what's true.
And slowly we achieved cognition, a half baked
wisdom, and then some time later on,
if fortunate, a little recognition.
But where did magic go?

Now looking through the looking glass of time,
how great, how different your perceptions were!
So frenzied in a whirlwind of impressions, when
dinner guests looked mad as hatters, and lime
trees were aglow.

Few things are perfect even for the lucky,
as for the wretched, one could say that
fantasy is only for defense. With that one,
I protest, even in noblest or the basest
of surroundings when one is young all things no
matter how mundane contain a marvel,
and marvel shields you from the pain of life
until you're thrust into the world
and there are still more lessons
to be learned.

Just like a Christian monk who
peeking through the trees of a green grove
and inside woods alight with fires
sees pagans naked in an orgy
begins to wonder why he joined the clergy
and why he had to leave the world.
Or simply put, when did he lose the sense of
sense that in his childhood used to make his
every living moment so intense and such a
mystery, which fear and prayer, fear of God
but moreso fear of death, have
now so dreadfully replaced?

The hatters are now dead, as are the parents.
The castle of your room is empty
and demolished. We start again with children
of our own and do it for a selfish wish to spawn
more mystery which we ourselves have killed
or if not us, then circumstance of life.

A poor excuse, such is the cycle which
we know wanes and ebbs with tides
and which with bones and caskets, poetry and
such old reminiscences provides.

I MISS THE COLD WAR

I miss the black and white.
I miss Apartheid and Pol Pot,
Communism and genocide.
I miss living under the threat of
mutually assured destruction.
It was exciting,
and romantic, one could say.

I pine for the days when
Unter den Linden and Friedrichstrasse and
Alexanderplatz were off limits.
And for the days when poetry could
land you in prison.
I long for a walled city
in the twenty first century.
I wish there were more poets in jail.

I miss the concept of the revolving
restaurant on top of Strijdom Tower where
one could spin around, chewing on impala while
men land on their heads at the bottom of
John Vorster Square.

I miss the cities without billboards.
I miss dreaming about steamy, humid nights in
Lourenco Marques, Luanda,
or Nova Lisboa.

I miss imagining the sounds
of bullets in the night
and sounds of people screaming.
I miss not being one of the poor sods
standing on Avenida Quatro de Fevereiro
waiting for a steamer to Portugal
with wife, baby, and refrigerator in tow.

Back in Europe it wasn't that exciting, we
had our noses stuck in cabbage, we'd given up.
But Asia, Africa, America, oh my! Cowboys and
Indians and rodeos! And good guys, and bad guys!
Noses and toes in cabbage we watched
the bad guys on a black and white screen
and thanked our luck. And we were proud
we weren't "oppressing the blacks".

I miss the bleeding and I miss the proxy wars.
I miss the blood and sand, and in the end,
I miss that history's remembrance is fleeting.
I miss conviction and convictions, one way
or another. And when I look at all of it today,
I miss the black and red more than I miss
the current grey.

MISTER GOD REGRETS (HE'S UNABLE TO LUNCH TODAY)

We soldier on, but who's it for?
To save the earth?
To aid the poor?
Realization comes too late.
It's over right as you awake and
though we die, we just make more.

The office workers bite into their sandwiches,
enjoy a fizzy drink at break out in the
open air of office plaza, while cars and
lives and buses pass us by.
"I want my lunch!"
"Dear!"

Meanwhile, Shiva dances.

Pointless to cry about
life's walking shadow,
the shooting arrow, meteor
or mountain, pick your luck.
Before you know,
the arrow's flown and
missed the apple, before you've
had a chance to duck.

Cynics we are, we learn the hard way
and a long time in the making.

And so we spawn and keep
traps shut: I've done my part, I've sown
what's needed to keep human race alive.

The kids will get it on their own.

GARDEN OF EDEN

Father Michael said to me in some few words
that meant "I'm done, peacefully waiting for
the other Michael, the Archangel...

I wait and bide my time for my demise and
trust in Christ".

He blessed me and my wife and in
the church, during coffee hour, (more like
cabbage hour for us Orthodox) he continued:

"I moved recently. Have some borscht, it is
delicious. We can discuss and I have so much
more to tell. You see, I've changed
my house in for a much smaller flat, believe it
or not, I love it lots and right across the street
from a zoo!

It is as if we've come full circle, original sin began
in a garden, and now I've got the garden
in full view! Now we come back to God!
And when I see the stars in twilight flicker, I
know that I'm approaching Him anew!"

Father, Father, it's not only the lights that flicker,
but lives and eyes and lashes,
and ambulance sirens.

Dear Father, don't you know that
we all live inside a zoo?

And most of us are chickens
thrown to feed the tigers?
And poultry, pious or profane,
like you the former, me the latter,
wait for the salivating maw while we
enjoy the view.

THE FAT MAN AND THE TOILET SEAT

A fat man sat on our old busted toilet and
broke it completely. The weight of
his elephantine haunches
cracked the seat.

He was a poet, with white Beethoven
mane of hair, and hemorrhoids to spare.

I must have been around the age of ten and
all I did was laugh at his disgrace.
He didn't care, his dignity was history.
Neither did I. For I was sore that he
ate all the tasty Finnish herring in one gulp, and
hated him for not offering me even just one bite,
how with impunity and such bravado he
placed the glass jar right onto his plate and
dove right in.
And so I snickered quite maliciously
about his toilet fate.

He's dead now, but I still recall him well,
his boozy smell, his mane and basic poet's
charms, accoutrements like Gordon's vodka,
and sordid stories that he'd tell.

The fat old man would speak quite proudly of
how in his youth, a girl who loved him jumped
into the drink and drowned in Die Donau.
Or maybe in the Dniester, or was it

Die Moldau?

But far from mourning he would slurp
the pickled fish into his mouth, his
grey hair flowing from the breeze of
New York City garbage nights.

This fat old man wrote maritime poems,
the boundless expanse of the sea.
And many romantics do get wildly caught
with pants way down, despite the girls who
drowned.

Apart from talk of sunken brides
he'd sit and drink and chime about
the poet's lot and when completely hammered
he'd trundle to the toilet:
even a poet has an ass, and that night
I laughed when our dog jumped on the door to
interrupt him as he passed some new material.

How do we wish to be remembered?
With deeds, with thoughts, with memories we
can all applaud? And for a poet, how much more
dreadful would your station be to
be remembered for one squalid bit: about how
you were not allowed to shit in peace.

Now looking back, in fairness I often found him
sweet, despite how he ate my herring and when I
saw him falling off the toilet seat.

INTERLUDE: THE BLACK SEA

The sea is warm, warm...
And the ocean so cold, cold in its
distance and its size.

Sailors in Yalta would throw
watermelons off the boat,
"Here, catch!"
and they would land and shatter if you missed.

The sun looks warm, warm, but
outside it's cold, cold

The boundless expanse of the sea.
Life's an illusion but I pray
"Please, Lord, don't let my memories fade.
Memory's what the world is made from,
and what the world is made of".

Who knows what's coming next?
Who knew what happened, how
life turned into sweet hell.

And how the final act went from
the hour between dog and wolf into
something unspeakable and
then the curtain fell.

Beginning of act three, some time before the

coda, we saw your mother in the
pre-cemetery, she too was not so mad yet,
but this woman had a special way of
making horrors sweet.

As if she found it funny, I always hated it
the way she spoke like that and so she started,
smiled with her remaining teeth in sterile
hospital of the nursing home,
much like death row where your cellmate's body
would be carted out each week and replaced with
a new one, she said
"What should I tell you? Once upon a time,
there lived Tonya. She had a daughter, Julia...."
The rest was too much for me to hear, the way
she said it.

I found my birth tags that you kept in a box
and treasured. You were a new mother once,
and you are still a mother...

Are memories the only thing that's real?

We lick the boots and
the sea licks the shores.

It also makes me fear for me,
and wonder which act I am in:
two or three?

And the sea is warm, warm...
And life is long, long...

And we risked limb and life
to come here,
build a future
which collapsed before completion.

Such is the immigrant song:
How long can you rest on your laurels
before the house of cards you built
is demolished and torn down?

CHRISTMAS IDYLL

On my first Christmas in America, I, mouth
agape, stared at the vitrines in amazement
and how idyllic then it seemed even while
stepping over homeless dregs so rank with filth
and bestial, hiding in a snowbank
poised to rape. The truth was brutal and
counterpoint against the whirligigs of
B. Altman's displays. This back in nineteen
hundred seven seven.

And yet these Dickensians scenes were better,
for back in Moscow we'd have wept
when there was talk of past times when
clementines could be bought at the shop
to be strung on a string around the tree.
The angels would come down and see
and sing, and people wept for times past which
most of them only knew from old novels.

Much of this talk had to be clandestine, and with
informers everywhere, my parents
whispered things into my ear which now in
retrospect sound like Eastern Europe's melting
pot of marzipan and guillotine,
the window dressings bathed in
blood as uniforms removed the cross but threw
the bourgeoisie a bone: a dead fir tree.
The way Saint Paul threw us a dead god.

I am reminded of the ending of the Nutcracker,
that final coda with the choral singing
feels like the swan song of a family
comfortable in their celebration: sweets,
chestnuts, tangerines on trees,
champagne and healthy burning fireplace,
the ones who don't see the reality and
go on with their lives while
right below their windows, a crowd
is forming, sharpening their knives.

SORROW OF FOOD

Hot, delicious pizza!

Individual pastry, 99 cents!

Don't forget the bread and milk!

Eggs on sale, $1.99 a dozen.
Welfare allots four fresh bananas for the baby
per month in California.

And "Nutrition Guide for New Mothers on
Raising a Healthy Infant" (Moscow, 1968),
discovered in 2008.

Food, glorious food.
We break bread, make friends.
Without nourishment we'd be dead
but we're all dying nonetheless.
Even the famous fan, Freddie Exley, on his
deathbed, asked not for alcohol but for a
"fresh strawberry yogurt".

The innocence in eating is that
everyone must eat and
we'll do anything in order to obtain it.
We'll steal the last stolen potato squirreled
in our bunk mate's striped pajamas
before he gets to snort some Zyklon B.

Come on, the old refrain is better him than me.

Meanwhile, for me, the innocence is lost.
No longer any thing that can be called
a simple pleasure, so I look wistfully at
subway ads for food banks, at the hobos
picking our hair covered crusts, at notices
for the assistance programs to
make the poor healthy so they can have
a healthy child.

I fill my guts, I don't break bread.
I have no final supper planned.
I am too filthy to be fed.
I'm way too bitter and too trenchant
to accept a Sacrament
and subway cars still pass me by
and carry on.

Starving, I suffocate and
I don't mean entombed,
covered in cork and
cookie crumbs in moustache
reminiscing about Swanns...

I mean, we starve and
thirst, because we are the ones!

WE ARE THE ONES

"How beautiful it all is", said
Theophanes the Greek, but
here I have to speak to add my own.
The beauty's not enough.
We need to fuck things up.

Come and examine, look and
rejoice at handiwork of God!
The untold myriad of mysteries, so
many birds, so many beasts, so many
unexpected twists of life unfold.

And then there's man...

I said it once, I'll say it twice,
I hate us more than beans and rice!
It's true now for round two,
I'll preface it again:
We love to fuck things up!

We love to shit right where we eat, for
each "storybook castle"
(there's one in every town in Europe)
has a certain history, which we collect as
part and parcel of our past, and drool and
wet our pants in the museums.

And in between our fine achievements, in
the basements, we stash other works of

progress and inventions, such as our instruments
for gouging eyes, something
for being broken on the wheel,
and persecution's
something we've perfected.
Who knows when you'll be werewolf next?

A pine forest in Spain, a birch grove in the
fields of Russia, the beauty will not do.
We have to own it and possess it, make it
our own by pissing on it too.

To saturate the grass with suffering and blood,
it's not enough to see the marvel of
creation, it needs a bit of added dash,
to brand everything with our burning poker
and when the chores are over we
can stuff our face.

We are God-Emperors of Hell,
exterminating heathens, enemies and
every blade of grass which
threatens us.
Then we build castles and
believe we're safe and smug.

What silly thoughts!
We're dust!
We are not kings, we're jesters!
We just draw moustaches on Mona Lisas!

For time and nature, two twin sisters,
both silent and both vengeful,
stand back and bide their time
as we demolish life divine.
Their wait is patient but it's they who
always have been in control,
they look upon our folly, pass the days,
they sew and knit from dusk to dawn and
passing time they wait until our castles
crumble, so they can take back
what is rightfully their own.

WE ARE

      THE ONES,

             And I'M....

      ...THE GIRL!

             (THAT FUCKING SLUT)

PEEK

A

BOO!

Yes, again...

I'm back, and now my ass is clean. You've been washing it since before you hit your teens!

           FUCK OFF!

           I TOLD YOU ONCE

        I TOLD YOU TWICE

          I HATE ME MORE

    THAN
            BEANS AND RICE

  AND MAN DO I FUCKIN

HATE YOU!

Go on, go on...
I've heard it all before.
Wha a bore your life is and yet
you cling. Unbelievable. You see I'm whispering
now, just so you can talk...

        THEN LET ME TALK!

I AM THE GIRL!

I am the girl who stepped on bread.
I didn't mean to, but I did,
and selfish, trodding on the loaf
and disrespecting life, I chose to sin
and now I bleed while
wingless flies and furious invertebrates
are covering my eyes.

I am the girl whose vanity and pride
took hold of me and cast aside
all decency. I pay the price, though
nothing new: self loathing is and
always has been me.

I am the girl who threw the bun into the mud
and used heavenly gift of food as just a brick
so that I wouldn't sully dainty shoes
and filth now rips into my sides and
there is nothing left in hell to lose.

But I had never ripped the wings off flies
I found no pleasure in the suffering of
other creatures. In fact, once as a child I cried
thinking that even Stalin, when his fangs weren't
dripping blood, would suck upon a chicken leg
and smile and maybe even say a prayer in thanks
for simple pleasures that
some simple taste provides.
He was a priest by training, after all.

So here's my plea to you, oh Lord!
I threw the bread into the mud, this I admit,
but is it really one strike and you're out?
The world is not just flawed,
it's bitter and it's brittle.
Forget the bread I threw into
the mud, and try to meet me
in the middle.

                What do you know?
                Don't you see now, that
                everything you ever did
                and everything you
                know is wrong?

I want to go BACK!

                WHERE TO?

You know quite well!

                To where I dwell?
                You're there right now!
                Talking about "worlds",
                writing greasy poetry,
                waxing nostalgic for
                a pimply faced slut or
                some other fat cunt?
                Holding on to ghetto
                memories?

There was a bridge outside my window
but I had nowhere to drive to.

                Drive all you want now!
                You can travel all you
                want for free!

ALMOST DONE! LET ME FINISH!

DREAM TRAVELS

The airlines have reduced their prices
but still too much for me to pay.
Cheap means so little,
when you have little or none.
Lucky for me, deep sleep
allows me cheapest travel all around the globe,
with lots of leg room on my king sized mattress
in the black night when
day is done.

Sometimes I dream I live in England,
its moist green magic in the mist, and
Jack in the Green hiding right
behind each oak tree,
pointing out strangest marvels,
like underground rivers of
London and other
wonders there for me to see.

My atelier in Mayfair's in a mews house,
I'm famous and well off, a painter or
perhaps even a writer, believe it or not!
The future's never seemed so bright...
Then I awake.

Sometimes I dream I live in Italy again.
This time not in the cemetery known as Rome
but on some sunny isle, Sicily or Sardinia.
In between swims I meditate on when

Aeneas or St Paul got stranded in a storm
and crashed on these same shores.
I sit on the white terrace and rack brains
trying to find a rhyme for "orange".

Rarely I dream that I'm back where I came from,
where under necks the swans are cut.
A place quite famous for its progeny:
some of the biggest cunts and charlatans
the world has ever seen.
In other words, people like me.

On sweetest nights I dream I still live
in California and I'm on set, making a film.
I watch the actors speak my words
and animate the actions I saw
in my mind.
I watch my writing come to life
as I imagined it, but satisfaction
comes to rude awakening when sun begins
to bang against the blinds.

Life's not just short but it gets
shorter by the second.
I rub my eyes and think of all the places
I would like to visit, while
staring at LA's brown sky.

No need for boarding pass or ticket.
No need to scrimp and save.

In padded casket's when
I'll finally fly first-class
out of this thicket,
while yellow palm trees sway over my grave.

It IS cheap to fly, especially right off your balcony!

STOP!

NO!!!

WAIT FOR IT!

Oh how we waited for something to happen,
checked whorrorscopes, coffee grinds, saying to
ourselves next year is going to be great!

Im Augenblick, Nick will return...

But how will we survive?

The Way of the World!
The way we always did!

And the stars will burn and
shine. I know, pedestrian metaphor...

And pedestrians will wake up,
rain or shine, and go to work.

And they'll compare notes with one another
about which doughnut is more tastier.
They'll talk about it in the elevator.

And they'll make mental notes, at
funerals or weddings.

Will compare notes about which
bread and egg sandwich tasted better
from the Egyptian fast food truck.

And they will come down.

Or come upstairs with bagels
for the staff, remember when their
bellies were heavy with life...

Too late my dear, it's
a new phase.

Oh phase, oh what a phase, but
some of us are just unfazed.

He'll love another one eventually,
this you should know!

So love me!

I can't.... I wish... I do....

And towers come on down,

And MELTING!

While humans dig claws into neck
and scream:
"You're wrong!
It's OUR turn now!"

Two hundred blocks up north,
it's meaningless to us.

We're talking and we think...

Your son will only be your son
for some such time.

Let him be!

The way of the world.

LET
        IT

                COME

                          DOWN!

Now we go West, for now we're through
with Europe yet again,
and all we have left now is kindling.

Another heartbreak and another joke,
one after other yet again.

                        Oh come on dear,
                        surely you've kindled.

The cycle's coming to an end...

                        That's true. We now
                        approach the ocean
                        and the desert. It's your
                        home now and you will
                        never go back to the
                        places you pine for.

You're right.
I despise you but you do
speak the truth....

Sometimes...

THE DESERT IS OUR HOME

The desert is our home now.
We thirst, and though we have the
freezing cold ocean and DWP
and the AC and pools out in Palm Springs and
Santa Ana winds, and pools and pools, we're in
the Desert, I mean the desolation.

The way the eyes are blinded
by the sun when we can party from
beaches to empires, pass out, get up, walk out
without seeing another soul for miles.

Although we might see people here and there
it's just a glimpse of spectres.

As in all deserts, we the nomads,
homeless, starve.
Moving along to the next watering hole, eyes
filled with sand and lust and information,
while in our own brown Timfucktoo,
cities of mud are every day erected.

And we have our own Reguibat who
love to cut out tongues, leaving
interpreters of human folly not
just mute but leave us as a plaything,
a muted human doll who's left only
to dream that he can scream.

Order! Silence! Profit! The cynicism
so snide but these are all just
distant episodes that time puts in
her pocket and waits until the worlds collide.

Can I be your little prince, oh star, oh pilot?
Sod off, I say! I'm off, returning to my bed.
Each night I go back to my own cozy and sordid
little planet. I like it here, that's where I'll stay!

And by the way, keep that damn
fox away!

Backtrack to the grog and the fog....

Chico runs back into the flat on McAllister,
back from the Welfare office, opens up a bag of
English muffins, carton of eggs,
a block of government cheese.
"Hey, just got my welfare check AND
my food stamps!"
Starts scrambling ovums, after a night of
scrambling ovaries and frying brains now
toasting muffins, shoveling them down,
"Fawk spwit" he manages to mouth
and then cracks himself up, so hungry.
Poor kid spent all his money on 40s and drugs.

Yes, his name actually was Chico.
He wasn't Chicano.
I think he was Lebanese.
Chico is not a Sea People name as far as I recall.

The janitor of the Russian church across
the street takes a smoke break and asks me
"How can anyone live in New York?
People there live like shit! Work for nothing!"
He spits and goes inside
to finish tidying up for Christ.
No bonding between me and him.
We spoke in the same language, but he,
this Gentleman from San Francisco, had grown
disdainful of New Yorkers, and probably
was thinking "They're all Jews".

Taking care of St John of Shanghai,

San Francisco and the East.
And grumbling about it quite a bit.

Soon enough, I had to leave.
I had enough of Frisco's duplicity.
We drove non-stop, taking turns driving, taking
turns dropping acid, we got a speeding ticket
outside of Chicago,
doing 120 in a Mercury station wagon that
groaned with all my earthly possessions.

I let Chico off in Philly, and crossed the bridges
by myself. I thought I'd never left.
That's how I tried to escape false promises,
from falling in the sea just for a little while,
until I saw that for one Lady Liberty,
there is an oceanful, or city full of Tralalas,
and that you have to watch your back
against the Harry Whites and
Harry Blacks.

                                        CO ?
                                              DA!?

        Let me finish!

                                              Get a job!

        The way you got a different suit?

                                              You betcha!

        Last one, ok?

THE MAN IN THE SEERSUCKER SUIT

I.

I have a brand new lover now.
He is bald, young, and pink.
Polite but with disdainful scowl.
He has an ocean for a pool in which
all swimming is Verboten:
his way of getting back at others.

I touch his heart but yet he too
is just as cruel as past romances.
I'd like to offer him my all
but his love isn't true.
He has much bigger fish to fry,
has money on his mind and
wears a fancy gold and white
seersucker suit.

I know he's teasing and I should exclaim
at least if not "Oh what a joke" then say
"What pain", finding myself again
in an embrace of geographic cure,
which is again debunked.
Geography might change but still manure
is manure, and every bright new place
so beckoning with hope will
always have to leave a space
under the table for a fat iguana.

He left me but he hasn't kicked me out,
I don't know where to go just now.
And where is he?
Why did he leave me?

II.

I've searched and think I've found the place
where this young man in fact resides, but
I'm confused and wonder why he chose a slum!
Bat wings neatly tucked in, he sits atop an old
Masonic Lodge, down by MacArthur Park.

Questions pop up, here's two or one:
For starters, is he really young?
And will he speak some Proto-Slavic to imitate
my Mother's tongue or
sprinkle holy water on my
burning eyes until all is revealed and
I am pushed and break my
neck falling down steps in Echo Park?

I can't see clearly now. My head's a mess.
And far from me to be the one
who'll find out what he thinks,
but I'll confess, I find his presence
comforting and sametime, how I dread
and fear this fine young chap.
I'll call him Pink for now, so I will christen him
in homage to his baby cheeks.

He is a nice young lad with
shirts pressed by most talented
of foreign tailors: hardly a crease,
but that is outward, the fact is that
he spreads disease, I've learned.
I've heard reports of him stumbling around
all neighbourhoods in town, and in
the gloaming, Pink's shirts appeared quite sullied,
dredged with mire, but he's still roaming,
in my dreams, and those of newcomers,
offering riches in exchange for
very unprotected love.

III.

How he taunts me! Such a cruel paramour!
I weep and soon after I fall asleep,
the nightmares wake me and I scream.
My Lord, this man just will not stop!
All your demands I'd heed but now my man is
gone, I sound and feel
like teenage hustler in need!
Where is he when I need him?

Seersuckers at just fifteen bucks in the
back pages of the Readers Digest rip
themselves right up from ads and breaking
free, fold paper into airplanes, pinions,
and even follow me to San Francisco:
old sailor's town of winos and opinions.

I don't care much for hippies, fog and hookers,
or seals and buffalos looking as dazed as
homeless lunatics in the Panhandle of
Rotten Gate Park.
The views are great, I'll give you that
but I still fear the dark and
that damn suit!

The Angel of Apocalypse stands
fast, feet firmly planted on the earth,
and delegates his delegates as needed.
They've got their work cut out for them
but Pink has got a cushy job,
for suckers are so many!

It's his realm down here as well,
and all he needs is just a little lolly,
one that he dangles by your tongue
and laughs while hanging to the trolley
waiting just for the right time to push you off.

IV.

Why should we care about decay?
It is our nature to start rotting once we're born.
But here with screenplays, palms, cosmetic
dentistry, agents, fantasies and riches and all the
things you've dreamt of back in greyer pastures,
the medicine goes down like syrup.
We swallow and we play on railroad tracks.

The views, don't let's forget about the views!
Pink knows much better than the Californians
that ocean vistas and Pacific sun will
still be here forever when we're gone.

"Now would you like a sucker, sucker?"
He grins his sparkling new teeth,
the filthy little fucker, pulls up a chair and glass,
and guiding burnt out eyes towards the horizon,
murmurs, snot nosed:
"Look and see! No better place
on earth for you" and, hissing, adds "or me!"

We lift up sunglasses and squint
and struggle to believe Pink's lies that
this is actually our home and listen
to his old used car salesman's technique
when he assures us that the ocean's warm.

All right, Pink, you win.

                        I always do!

                        Good night...

www.ingramcontent.com/pod-product-compliance
Lightning Source LLC
Chambersburg PA
CBHW031454040426
42444CB00007B/1099